Contents

Routemasters	5
The 73	12
Pottering About	14
Lost Liveries	20
Edmonton Green	24
After Dark	26
Bridges	30
I-Bus	34
E400s	35
The 185 Goes Bust	39
Step Entrance Farewell	42
Route March	47
Snow	54
Darting Around	58
Double Deckers	63
Marble Arch	72
Golden Jubilee	78
Single Deckers	82
London's Olympians	90
'38' Changes	95
Training	98
Sightseeing	102
Help	104
Metrobuses	106
Hill Climbing	112
The Irish Connection	114

Introduction

Since the turn of the century, the London bus scene has remained as colourful and varied as it was during the end of the 20th century. Until now. TfL's push towards 100% low-floor operation across the network has been achieved and now the 100% red rule has come into operation, taking away a variety of individual liveries that added a splash of colour to the capital's streets. Back in the mid-1980s, when London's bus routes were first placed out to competitive tender and new operators and liveries came onto the streets of London, many enthusiasts were unhappy about the loss of the all-red London Bus. The reverse is the case today with many of us bemoaning the loss of variety. It seems that what goes around, comes around. And in true British style, we are just not happy.

'London's Buses in the 21st Century' takes a look at the changes the capital has seen over the past eleven years. Well eleven years and ten weeks to be exact. Operators that have come and gone, lost liveries, the end of step entrance buses and the introduction of Hybrid vehicles all make the start of the 21st Century as varied and interesting as the last. The so-called 'Borismaster' also made a tentative step into service and only time will tell whether it will be a success or a hugely expensive white elephant.

Photography-wise, I have been 100% digital since 2000 and as technology has improved over the years, no doubt the reproduction quality of the images will also have improved. If one or two images are not 100% perfect, please accept my apologies. Ken Carr, of Visions International, has done sterling work to bring them up to standard for printing but in many cases these are the only photos I have of a particular type, livery or operator and are, therefore, an important part of this book.

As with all good books, I could not have done it alone and should mention the following:

Ken Carr for giving me the opportunity to present my work in printed form, for putting up with my constant emails and for trying but not always succeeding, to tell me what should or should not be included. And of course for designing the book.

Websites and publications were invaluable in providing information about routes, vehicles and dates. Bus Lists on the web (http://www.buslistsontheweb.co.uk/) and London Bus Route Histories (http://www.londonbuses.co.uk/) were used most frequently and are highly recommended as valuable sources of information. A Google search would often provide a link to other required information. And publications such as Visions International's 'London Bus Guide' (http://www.visionsinternational.biz) and 'The London Bus and Tram Fleetbook' from LOTS have also been worth their weight in gold (http://www.lots.org.uk/). Last, but by no means least, is the excellent 'London Bus Page' by Matthew Wharmby at http://www.londonbuspage.com/.

That just about brings my introduction to an end. When writing the text captions I have tried to ensure that dates and other information are correct, hopefully I have succeeded. All photographs in this book are my own and I have had enormous pleasure in choosing the ones to use and writing the captions. It certainly brought back some good memories and hopefully this book will do that for you too. I have worked as a bus driver for the past twenty five years, fourteen of those in London and this has enabled to me take a variety of photos whilst at work, as well as out and about across London. Happy memories indeed.

Peter Horrex
Enfield, Middlesex
April 2012

THE ROUTEMASTERS

On Friday 9th December 2005 the last Routemaster buses ran in service in London, route 159 having the honour of being the very last route. The type can still be seen in London on Heritage routes 9 & 15 which duplicate part of the normal service on those routes in Central London. We can also still see Routemaster buses in London not on normal passenger service. The following set of photographs shows Routemasters at work pre 2005, on routes 9 & 15 and on other duties.

A typical scene in Oxford Street in February 2002 as Routemasters dominate. RML2681 (SMK681F) works route 98 whilst RML2532 (JJD532D) heads in the opposite direction on route 6. Both of these Willesden based Metroline routes lost their RMs in March 2004. They were replaced by sixty-nine Volvo B7TL Transbus Presidents.

RML2430 (JJD430D) from Holborn enters Oxford Street at the Tottenham Court Road junction, bound for Willesden bus garage. Heading in the opposite direction is RML2716 (SMK716F) in a black advertising livery on route 38.

5

Arriva's RML2572 (JJD572D) passes Clapham Common. Taken in 2002, Routemasters had just two years left working on route 137, which was converted to driver only or one person operation (OPO) in July 2004. The replacements were DB250 Wrightbus Geminis.

Another view of the '137' with Arriva's RML2549 (JJD549D) at Clapham Common. When the Brixton based Routemasters came off this route the peak vehicle requirement (PVR) was increased from twenty-eight to thirty-four.

London's Buses in the 21st Century

Oh to see this again, a trio of Routemasters in the bus station at Victoria, before the bus station had its roof removed. Arriva's RML2742 (SMK742F) waits to depart on route 73, whilst in the middle RML2709 (SMK709F), part of the Stagecoach fleet, prepares to work a journey on route 8. Bringing up the rear is another Arriva Routemaster, this time RML2354 (CUV354C), on route 38. Pure nostalgia.

Route 94 (Piccadilly Circus to Acton Green) is a relatively young route, being introduced in September 1990, replacing the withdrawn section of route 88. Making the turn into Oxford Street from the stand at Oxford Circus is London United's RML2722 (SMK722F). Operated by Shepherds Bush garage, the route converted from RMs to Dennis Trident ALX400s in January 2004.

Approaching Putney Bridge Station in 2002 is London General's RML2461 (JJD461D) working route 22 to Putney Common. This Putney operated route lost its RMs in July 2005 on the same day that the garage's other remaining RM route, the 14, also lost its RMs. Both routes were replaced by Volvo B7/ Wrightbus Geminis.

A lovely sunny day in February 2002 as Stagecoach RML2311 (CUV311C) makes its way around Marble Arch, bound for Paddington on route 15. This route, operated out of Upton Park garage, finally lost its RMs in August 2003. They were replaced by Dennis Trident ALX400s. By the final day there were only five serviceable RMs left in service.

London's Buses in the 21st Century

Before the last Routemaster ran on the 159, two 'heritage' routes, both utilising Routemasters, had started running in November 2005. These were primarily created to ensure that tourists could still see and ride on London's iconic bus. Routes 9 & 15 were chosen, but the RMs only run on parts of these routes in Central London.
First have the contract to operate route 9 from Westbourne Park garage and initially they ran from Albert Hall to Aldwych, but in November 2010 this was changed to Kensington High Street to Trafalgar Square. Here, RM204 (204CLT) enters Cockspur Street on the approach to Trafalgar Square on 14th July 2007.

The 'heritage' route 15 is operated by Stagecoach, out of West Ham garage. It operates between Tower Hill and Trafalgar Square. On 5th November 2011, RM1968 (ALD968B) negotiates the roundabout at Trafalgar Square to begin another eastbound journey. The route 9 RMs also use this roundabout to turn and this is the only place the routes overlap.

9

First's RM1650 (650DYE), carries fleet number SRM3 and has been in a number of liveries. On 14th July 2007 it passes along Cockspur Street painted in a livery carried during the Queen's Silver Jubilee in 1977.

Long after their supposed withdrawal it was often possible to see Routemasters at work on rail replacement duties. Archway is the location for this view of Blue Triangle's RM298 (VLT298) on 16th November 2006.

London's Buses in the 21st Century

Hundreds of Routemasters were preserved/saved. This means that it is commonplace to see RMs other than the heritage route examples, out and about on London's streets. Some are used on a commercial basis, others may appear as part of an enthusiast organised running day. One of the former category, RML2573 (JJD573D) has been outshopped in an over-all advertising livery for Capital FM and Windows 7 and is captured at Victoria during the evening of 4th December 2009.

The final shot in this section features RMA48 (NMY631E) at the Nags Head in Holloway Road on 7th April 2007. It was being used by BBC London for promotional work. Incidentally, RMA48 was new to British European Airways in January 1967.

11

THE 73

Way back in 1949 Route 73 operated between Stoke Newington and Richmond and by the late 1950s had been extended to Hounslow garage. In 1983 the route was cut back to Hammersmith, before being cut back even further in August 1988 by being diverted at Hyde Park Corner to Victoria, the withdrawn section being covered by new route 10. During the first decade of the 21st century, a host of vehicle types have worked on the route.

Above: At the start of the new millennium, it was a Routemaster route using buses from Tottenham garage. On 26th June 2004, Arriva's RML2292 (CUV292C) departs from Victoria bus station.

Left: Here's something we're not likely to see again, Routemaster buses lining Oxford Street as far as the eye can see! Taken from the top deck of another Routemaster, we see RML2434 (JJD434D) heading towards Victoria in 2003.

In common with all crew operated routes in London, the 73 was converted in the late 1980s to OPO on Sundays. The '73' used Metrobuses from Stamford Hill for these workings. This shot, however, of M665 (KYV665X) being pursued by RML2569 (JJD569) in Oxford Street in 2002 was taken on a weekday. Busy, high frequency routes are prone to bunching, and the Routemaster we can see in the distance is also on route 73.

London's Buses in the 21st Century

In September 2004 route 73 succumbed to Bendybuses, operating from Lea Valley and yet another Routemaster route was lost. The route was also withdrawn between Seven Sisters and Tottenham. Like them or loathe them, the Bendybus was a part of the London bus scene for the best part of a decade. MA40 (BX04MYG) enters Oxford Street from Marble Arch in May 2009 heading for Seven Sisters.

Seven years after losing its Routemaster buses to the Bendybus, Mayor Boris Johnson continued his policy of converting all Bendybus routes back to double-decker operation. On conversion day, 3rd September 2011, brand new HV27 (LJ11EFT) departs Victoria, it is one of twenty Volvo B5L Wrightbus Hybrid buses allocated to the route alongside a batch of conventional Wrightbus Gemini 2s. All are based at Stamford Hill. The return to double-decker operation also saw the route terminate once again at Stoke Newington.

13

POTTERING ABOUT

A host of vehicle types have operated from Potters Bar garage, particularly during the late 1980s. With second-hand Volvo Ailsa's and Metrobuses working alongside standard London Transport Metrobuses and new Scanias purchased for route 263 in 1989, workings from the garage provided the opportunity for some interesting photos. However, here we are concerned with more recent times and the images show the variety of types over the past decade.

It is hard to imagine that route 217 was operated by single-decker buses, but indeed it was. The route came to Potters Bar in June 1990 and was worked with double-decker Metrobuses before being converted to single-decker Dennis Darts in July 1998. It reverted to double-decker operation in June 2003. EDR27 (P303MLD), a Plaxton bodied Dennis Dart, is seen in Potters Bar in 2002, alongside EDR17 (P292MLD) which is set to work a journey on route 326, a route still worked by Metroline but not from Potters Bar garage.

Marshall bodied Dennis Darts were also a common type at Potters Bar garage. DMS9 (R709MEW) was new in February 1998 to MTL London Northern and is seen here on a short working of route 234 at East Finchley on 15th May 2007. Route 234 was created at the end of the 1980s to cover the northern section of the 134, which was cut back from High Barnet to Friern Barnet. Initially the 234 ran from High Barnet to Archway, duplicating routes 43 and 134 between Friern Barnet and Archway station, using double-decker buses, but was subsequently converted to single-decker operation and diverted via Muswell Hill and then Fortis Green to East Finchley. It now terminates at Highgate Wood.

London's Buses in the 21st Century

Keeping buses maintained is a continuous process, with regular servicing and minor repairs. Elevated above head height inside Potters Bar garage in 2002 is another Marshall bodied Dart, this time DMS20 (S520KFL), with its engine removed.

By virtue of its outlying location in relation to London, Potters Bar garage has operated some non TfL routes, as well as commercial services. Introduced in October 1986, route 310a operated an hourly service between Enfield Town and Hertford, alongside routes 310 & 311. M1250 (B250WUL) collects passengers in Enfield in 2002, just a year before Metroline withdrew its 310a service.

One of the Scanias originally used on route X43 (from Holloway garage, and then Potters Bar), is S16 (J816HMC), seen here as an unusual working on route 231 in Enfield Town in 2002, the route at the time being scheduled to be operated by Marshall bodied Dennis Darts. The 231 is another route that came to Potters Bar garage from Leaside's Enfield garage in June 1990, and was worked by Metrobus double-decker buses until being converted to single-decker Dennis Darts at the same time as the 217, in July 1998. It reverted to double-deck operation in June 2003 and was worked by Presidents as was the 217.

15

Some of the Alexander bodied Volvo Olympians within Metroline migrated to Potters Bar and were mainly used on the commercial routes 84 & 242. AV38 (S138RLE) is seen on the Rosedale Estate, Flamstead End, on a short working of route 242 in September 2007. Route 242 is not part of the London TfL network and therefore does not accept Oyster or Travelcards.

The Enviro200 has become the standard single-decker bus in London, albeit in varying lengths. A batch of the 10.8 metre, single-door version came to Potters Bar in the summer of 2008, for use on commercial routes 84 and 242. Sporting a digital destination display, these cannot work on any TfL route and the only destinations programmed into the system are those required for the above routes, plus the usual oddities such as 'Private', 'Metroline' and 'Not in Service' etc. In the summer of 2009, DEL856 (LK08DWL) leaves Waltham Cross on a glorious sunny day, bound for Cuffley Station on route 242.

London's Buses in the 21st Century

Routes 217 and 231 were won by London Northern in 1990 from what was then Leaside and the routes were operated from Potters Bar garage, although the 231 was subsequently lost to First in 2008. The 217, however, continues to operate from Potters Bar, and TP439 (LK03GGV), a Dennis Trident new in 2003 looks resplendent in the summer sun leaving Waltham Cross for Turnpike Lane on 2nd June 2009.

After five years and a day with First Capital, route W8 returned home to Potters Bar on 26th July 2003. For a short while Dennis Dart buses were used as it was a tight squeeze under the rail bridge at Edmonton Green for the new Tridents, although once the road was lowered beneath the bridge, double-decker buses were once again the norm. In June 2010, the driver of TP443 (LK03GHA) waits patiently whilst passengers alight at St Stephens Church in the Bush Hill Park area of Enfield.

Metroline has only twelve of the shortest 8.9 metre version of Enviro200, all are based at Potters Bar. They are used on routes 383 & 384. The 383 is a relatively new route, being created in July 1998 to cover the withdrawn section of route 326 between Barnet and Potters Bar. The route passed to Sullivan Buses in July 2003 but returned to Potters Bar five years later in July 2008. Numerically the last of the batch, DES802 (LK07ELO) is seen midway through its journey from Woodside Park to Barnet Spires in Netherlands Avenue, during February 2011.

During the night of 1st February 2009 London suffered one of its heaviest snowfalls for many years. Buses across London were taken off the road and few buses operated the following day, although as that day progressed, some services did start to see some sort of service. Potters Bar, however, was the exception, and no buses ran at all from here on the 2nd February. As can be seen in this view, the snow made manoeuvring buses a tricky task, and with even the main roads out of Potters Bar still covered in snow into the evening, it was deemed unsafe to try to run any buses. Three Enviro200s and three Tridents huddle together for warmth.

London's Buses in the 21st Century

In February 2009 route 263 was extended at its southern end beyond Archway to Holloway, Nags Head, and a batch of seventeen Enviro400 buses was allocated to Potters Bar for the take up of the new contract, replacing the Presidents which had previously worked the route. The first of these numerically, is TE935 (LK09EKP), seen here making the turn from Holloway Road into Camden Road at the end of its journey from Barnet Hospital on 8th April 2009 when it was just two months old.

Like the batch of DES buses previously mentioned, the entire batch of ten DSDs in the Metroline fleet is also based at Potters Bar. The buses were transferred in to enable the withdrawal of the older Marshall bodied Darts. New in 2002, these 9.3 metre Plaxton bodied Dennis Darts are allocated to route W9. DSD217 (LR02BFE) is the last of the batch and is pictured here at Highlands Village on 4th June 2010.

LOST LIVERIES

Since 2000 there have been many changes of operator, this and a plan to standardise bus liveries on TfL services have seen the multi-coloured approach gradually turn red. This section looks back at some of the operators who have now gone and the older liveries of those that still remain.

The T33 route was born in 2000, along with two other new routes, to link to the new Croydon Tramlink when it opened in May 2000. The T33 was just a renumbering of the existing 354 at its Croydon end. Awarded to the incumbent, Metrobus, we see Dennis Dart W334VGX on 28th July 2001 at West Croydon heading for Addington.

Capital Citybus was a Hong Kong based company formed in 1990 that operated services in east and north London. It was purchased by First in 1998. This is East Lancs bodied Dennis Dart, 716 (R716VLA) which was delivered to Capital Citybus in February 1998. This photo shows that it still carried its Capital Citybus livery as it departed Stratford bus station in April 2002, four years after being taken over by First.

London's Buses in the 21st Century

Route 209 was born on 8th March 1997, running between Mortlake and Hammersmith bus station. Two and a half years later, in October 2009, the route was converted to low-floor operation and awarded to Armchair. Late in 2004, Metroline acquired Armchair and the route is still operated by Metroline today. Armchair's Alexander bodied Dennis Dart T149AUA enters Hammersmith bus station on 1st May 2002.

Mitcham Belle took over the operation of route 200 on 26th June 2000, but it was lost to London General six years later. Dennis Dart W147WGT is pictured at Wimbledon on 28th July 2001.

21

The days of the MCW Metrobus were clearly numbered when this photograph of London United's M1266 (B266WUL) was taken at Hammersmith on 1st May 2002 on route H91. The H91 has used many different vehicle types during its 21 year life and was officially operated by low-floor Dennis Lance single-decker buses at the time this photo was taken.

Limebourne had commenced operation of route 344 in May 1999 from a base in Battersea using low-floor single-decker buses. The route was converted to Trident ALX400 operation in June 2002, a year after this photo of T410LGP, a Caetano bodied Dennis Dart, was taken at Clapham Junction. National Express, under the Travel London banner, took over Limebourne in 2004.

London's Buses in the 21st Century

Thamesway took over operation of route 191 on 4th May 1996, using Darts. It was swallowed up by First Group in September 1998. One of the former Thamesway Darts, 693 (K903CVW) shows off another variant of the First livery as it heads along Southbury Road, Enfield in February 2002.

A former National Express owned Travel London Optare Excel R412HWU is seen at Victoria working route 211 in July 2001. Travel London had won this route in 1998, but sold the operation to Limebourne in August 2000. The Excels were inappropriate for the loadings on the route but it took until November 2002 for Trident ALX400s to be introduced. Ironically, National Express's takeover of Connex (owners of Limebourne) in July 2005 saw the route operated by Travel London once again. Travel London was sold to Abellio in May 2009.

EDMONTON GREEN

Those of us who are young enough to remember the sit-com "Some Mothers do 'ave 'em", will remember the spiral stairs from the bridge above the bus station in Edmonton Green being used in one episode, as the accident-prone Frank Spencer has a few problems whilst on roller skates. But the bridge also served as a good vantage point for over-head shots of buses. Sadly, that is no longer possible, as a new bus station was completed in 2007 without the over-head bridge.

Taken from the aforementioned bridge, Arriva and First dominate this 2002 view of Edmonton Green bus station. The high volume of services using the bus station made it just a matter of time before it was redesigned.

The bridge above the old bus station is clearly visible in this view of First London's TN876 (T876KLF) departing at the start of its journey on route 191 to Brimsdown in 2002. In 2001 the 191 lost its Metrobus allocation in favour of low-floor Tridents. Today it is still possible to see a Trident working on the 191, although Enviro400s are the norm.

During the rather lengthy rebuild of the bus station (it was not completed until 2007) services had to pick up at two specially created bus stops on Hertford Road. On 5th March 2005 First London's VNL32297 (LK03NGV), a Volvo B7TL, departs at the start of its journey to Kings Cross on route 259. In 2010 the route received brand new Wright bodied Gemini 2 Volvo B9TLs.

London's Buses in the 21st Century

Metroline's Trident TP360 (LR52KWB) pulls out of the new bus station in July 2007 working the W8. This bus was new in 2003 and as Metroline retained this contract in July 2010, it may still be working the route in 2015.

Not all services pick up inside the bus station. Some, but not all, starting services have their first pick up point outside of the bus station, as in this view of Arriva's VLW40 (LJ51DJE), a Volvo B7TL with Wrightbus Gemini working route 144 on 6th May 2008.

25

AFTER DARK

Modern cameras, with their lack of grain at high ISO settings, make photography of buses at night possible without flash. This adds another dimension to the photographic opportunities available. Here is a selection.

Route 68 has a PVR of 21 vehicles and has been operated by Go-Ahead's London Central since April 2006. At Waterloo on 12th January 2007 is WVL243 (LX06EAE), a Gemini bodied Volvo B7TL.

On 23rd June 2007 Metroline took over operation of route 7 from First. SEL751 (LK07BBU), an East Lancs bodied Scania is stopped at the traffic lights adjacent to Oxford Circus tube station in December 2007.

London's Buses in the 21st Century

On 9th November 2010, East London's RM871 (WLT871) awaits departure from Charing Cross on heritage route 15, whilst a Go Ahead Volvo Gemini WVL122 (LX53AZP) will follow it on route 11.

Having succumbed to the ubiquitous Bendybus in October 2005, route 38 had a PVR of 42. On 7th November 2009 the route was converted back to double-decker operation, and the PVR jumped substantially to 70. On 9th December 2009 Arriva's DW222 (LJ59AEO) awaits its departure time at an unusually deserted Victoria bus station.

Having been turned short at Hyde Park Corner whilst working route 82, Metroline's Potters Bar based Enviro400, TE937 (LK09EKT) prepares to head back to North Finchley on 15th March 2010. At the time, this was an unusual working, the 82 was scheduled to be worked by Metroline's TPL class of Dennis Trident Presidents. Since its introduction in June 1986 the 82 has never changed hands, being worked from Finchley garage until its closure in 1993 when Potters Bar garage took over the allocation. A contract renewal in March 2012 saw Metroline retain the route, and proposed new Enviro400 buses are due to be introduced in due course.

Ex Bendybus route 29 also received Arriva's DW class, when the Bendybuses were withdrawn and double-decker operation returned on 26th November 2011. But, unlike the 38, the PVR only jumped from 29 to 42. On 30th November 2011 DW474 (LJ61CDU) collects passengers at Wood Green bound for Trafalgar Square.

London's Buses in the 21st Century

The present route 232 was born on 6th August 1994 to replace the withdrawn section of route 112 between Brent Cross and Wood Green. This route is another never to have changed hands, being worked initially from London Northern's Potters Bar garage before being transferred within Metroline to Cricklewood and then North Wembley. On the closure of North Wembley in 2009 the route was moved to Perivale West. MAN is not a common breed in London, although Metroline do have some that were purchased in 2007 with MCV Evolution bodywork. Here, MM785 (LK57EHV) heads through Wood Green on 30th November 2011.

Normally the domain of Arriva's DLA and DLP class DAF buses, here route 121 plays host to VLW122 (LF52UOV), a Volvo B7TL Gemini collecting passengers in Enfield Town on 8th December 2011. The 121 has almost always been operated out of Enfield (E) garage, although it has moved in and out of Palmers Green (AD) on more than one occasion.

BRIDGES

London, like most other cities, has its fair share of bridges. Here we have a selection of photos that show various types of buses at work in the capital over the past decade, with the common theme of having just passed under a bridge.

A pair of Potters Bar based Trident Presidents squeeze under the bridge at Edmonton Green station at work on route W8 on 16th April 2011. Showing its rear is TP440 (LK03GGX) heading towards Chase Farm Hospital, whilst TP454 (LK03GHY), a fire victim in late 2009, heads in the opposite direction to the Lee Valley Leisure Centre.

London's Buses in the 21st Century

Prior to its launch in 2002, route RV1 was promoted as the Riverside Bus, and proved hugely popular. The route has seen a variety of vehicle types. In 2002, Mercedes-Benz Citaro EC2011 (LT02NVY) passes through Waterloo, heading for Tower Gateway. Today the route uses Hydrogen fuel cell buses (alongside other types), as we shall see elsewhere in this book.

One of Metroline's Alexander bodied Volvo Olympians, AV33 (S133RLE), has just passed under the bridge at Golders Green underground station, working the lengthy route 260 in March 2002. On 28th June 2003 the route was cut back at its northern end between Golders Green and North Finchley, the withdrawn section being covered by new route 460.

210, (S210LLO) a Northern Counties bodied Volvo Olympian was delivered new to Capital Citybus and joined the First fleet after the 1998 take-over. In March 2002 it works route 341 at Waterloo. The bridge, built in the 19th Century, used to link the London & South Western Railway with the South Eastern Railway from Waterloo to Waterloo East; today it forms part of a walkway. This route had been operated by First since its introduction back in 1998, until October 2010 when the route was awarded to Arriva using new Enviro400s.

The rail bridge in Potters Bar is famous for a rather nasty train crash in 2002. Just over six years later, on 9th April 2008, Metroline's Enviro200 DEL853 (LK08DWF) has just passed under the bridge working route 84 to St Albans. At that time part of the 84, the Barnet to Potters Bar section, accepted TfL tickets, but this ceased in January 2012 and the route is now a complete commercial operation.

Arriva's Optare Solo 2470 (YJ06YRS) leads Enviro400 T40 (LJ08CUO) under the Northern Line bridges at East Finchley in April. With the exception of the 0645 departure from Golders Green (0700 on Sundays), the H3 runs an hourly service between 0900 and 1400 daily except Sundays.

London's Buses in the 21st Century

In the early stages of tendering route 298 was awarded to London Country in 1986, and since then has also been worked by Grey-Green and Capital Citybus before settling down with Arriva. DWL50 (LF52UOB), a DAF SB120 with Wrightbus Cadet bodywork, arrives at Potters Bar station working route 298 on 8th June 2006. In February 2012 the 298 passed to Sullivan Buses.

A 10.2 metre, Cricklewood based Enviro200, DE1026 (LK59AVO) passes under the bridge for Brondesbury station in the Kilburn area of north-west London in December 2010. Note the air conditioning unit on the roof.

33

I-BUS

One of the biggest changes to the way London's buses are controlled came in the 21st century with the introduction of ibus. On board displays inform the passengers of the route and the next stop as the bus approaches. These displays are accompanied by clear announcements from an automated system, particularly useful for visually impaired passengers. Buses are tracked by ibus controllers back at the home garage for the route concerned, and can be held back or pushed forward when the service requires it.

One of the on-board displays that show alternately the route number/destination of the bus and the next stop.

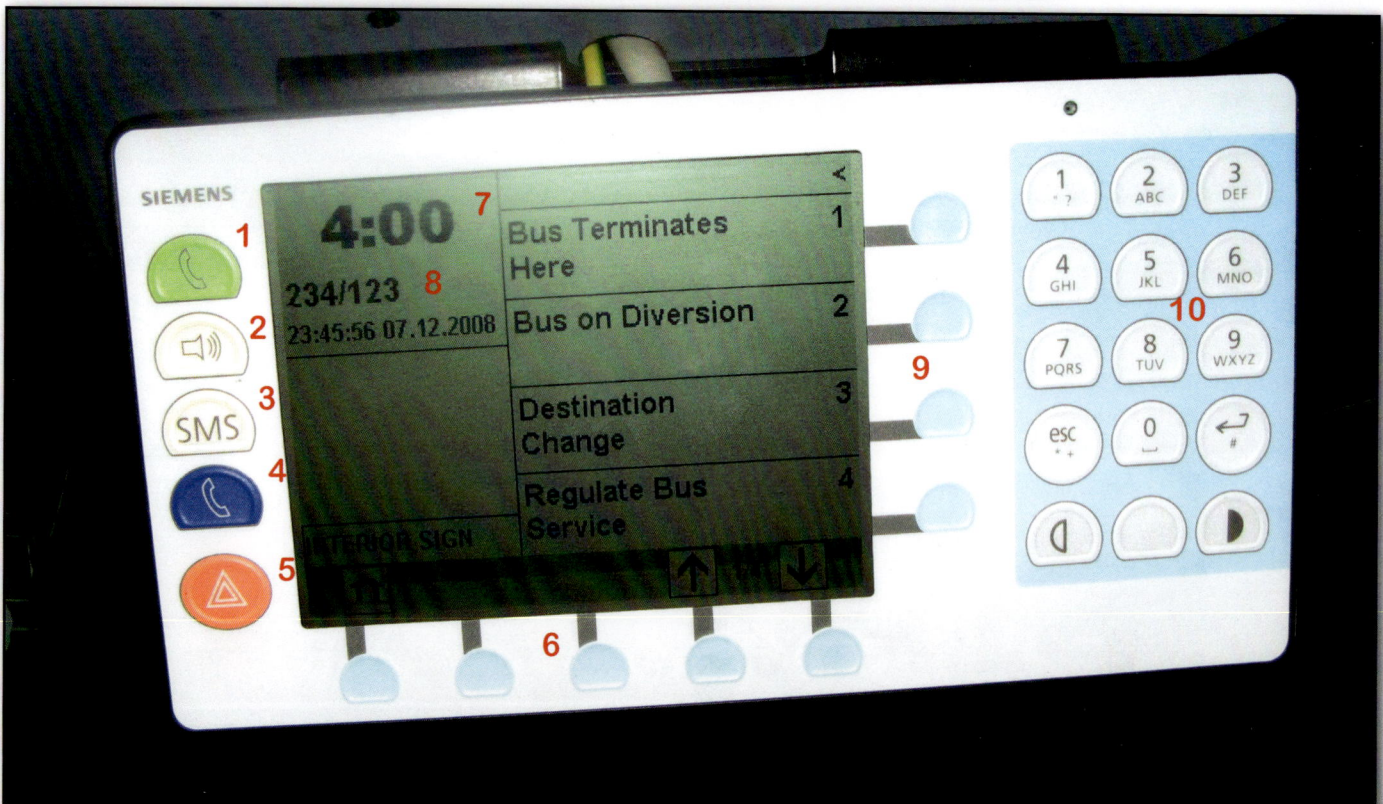

This is the driver's ibus screen which is used to programme in the route details at the start of the journey. The driver then has access to many functions he/she may need throughout the journey. Some of these are explained below.

1 - The green button makes a radio call to the home garage ibus control base.
2 - This button activates the on-board personal announcement system, enabling the driver to speak to all of the passengers.
3 - A range of pre-programmed text messages are available for the driver to send direct to their home ibus base.
4 - The 'code blue' button is for contacting Centrecomm* via the radio for non-emergency calls such as a travel enquiry.
5 - The 'code red' button is for contacting Centrecomm* when emergency assistance is required.
6 - These buttons access a variety of menus, depending on whether the driver wishes to set up the system, send messages etc.

7 - This part of the display changes to show the driver information relating to timekeeping. This particular image is showing the driver that there are four minutes remaining until departure time. If a + or – symbol is show the bus is either running late or early.
8 - This shows the route and running number. In this case route 234, running number (PB) 123.
9 - Once the menu has been selected using the bottom row of buttons, these side buttons are used to select the item the driver wishes to use. The up and down arrows at the bottom are used to scroll through the list of available items.
10 - The key pad is used to input details when required, such as the route number etc.

*Centrecomm is TfL's central communications team. It is independent of the individual operating companies and deals with emergencies, road closures etc, as well as offering instant assistance to road staff.

London's Buses in the 21st Century

Now a common sight on the streets of the capital, with over 1,000 in operation, the Alexander Dennis Enviro400 first appeared in late 2005 when Stagecoach took delivery of LX55HGC, named 'Spirit of London', as a replacement for the Trident lost in the July 2005 bombings. The first to enter service were with Metroline in January 2006.

Metroline took over operation of route 24 in November 2002 and introduced Enviro400s on it in 2006. However, they lost it to London General in 2007 and they also use Enviro400s on the route. At Trafalgar Square on 15th February 2009 is E1 (SN06BNA), numerically the first of London General's Enviro400s.

In June 2008 route 231 passed from Metroline to First. Brand new Enviro400s based at Northumberland Park, took over, replacing Trident Presidents. On 1st September 2010 First's DN33532 (SN58CEX) heads south along Great Cambridge Road at Trinity Avenue.

Marble Arch, busy as ever with traffic, is the setting for this fine view of Metroline's TE882 (LK08DXU) heading for Victoria on route 16 on 28th January 2009. Since the route tendering programme started back in the mid 1980s the 16 is another of those routes that has never changed hands, remaining at Cricklewood with Metroline.

First's DN33536 (SN58CEX) enters the one-way system in Enfield from Southbury Road on 4th October 2010. This bus was delivered new two years earlier in October 2008, and E400s are now the norm on the 191, although older low-floor buses do appear.

London's Buses in the 21st Century

In the same month that it was announced that National Express had agreed to sell Travel London to the Abellio Group, May 2009, 9431 (LJ09CAU) works route 40 on London Bridge.

Potters Bar garage had its first intake of Enviro400s in February 2009 for the new contract on route 263. The type does stray regularly onto other routes from PB, as in this view of TE938 (LK58KHC) on route W8 at Bush Hill Park on 8th November 2010.

37

The first hybrid version of the Enviro400 pitched up in early 2009 and now over 100 are in operation. TEH1113 (LK60AJY) crosses Waterloo Bridge as it approaches the end of its journey on route 139 on 25th April 2011.

Long overdue new buses are finally in use on Arriva's route 279, which runs between Waltham Cross and Manor House. T225 (LJ61CFU) leads T230 at Edmonton Green on 28th February 2012 at a time when only a handful of the type had entered service on the route.

London's Buses in the 21st Century

THE 185 GOES BUST

Route 185, between Lewisham and Victoria, was operated by Durham Travel Services trading as London Easylink on behalf of TfL when the company called in the receivers. Buses were impounded and the service stopped immediately, leading to TfL asking Blue Triangle to arrange emergency cover. This brought a whole variety of vehicles in varying liveries back into London.

Route 185 was operated by Plaxton President bodied Volvo B7TL buses but in August 2002, days before the collapse of the company, Scania YU02GHK was working the route at Victoria. This bus was part of a batch delivered just the previous month for operation on another TfL route, 42, so this is an extremely rare working of this type on the 185.

Blue Triangle's ex London Leyland Titan, WYV4T looks immaculate as it leaves Victoria for Lewisham in November 2002 one of many buses used between August 2002 and April 2003 when Blue Triangle ran the emergency cover.

Ex London Metrobuses were common during this operation. Arriva's GYE399W which was allocated to 'The Original Tour' service was roped in to help out. Here seen just after arrival at Victoria.

Carousel Buses' ex London Metrobus KYV737X was drafted in to help and is also seen at Victoria in November 2002.

London's Buses in the 21st Century

Redroute Buses was also involved in providing buses for the emergency service, in this case Metrobus WYW49T. This was certainly an interesting few months for the enthusiast.

In 2003 East Thames Buses took over permanent operation of the 185 from its base at Belvedere. P343ROO is an East Lancs bodied Volvo Olympian, new to Harris Bus, and is pictured here in Lewisham bus station in April 2003. In 2009 East Thames was sold to Go Ahead (London General) and the company won the contract for the route for five more years in October 2009. It is now generally worked by Volvo B7TL Geminis.

41

STEP ENTRANCE FAREWELL

TfL's drive towards accessible low-floor buses across the network has been achieved. Here we take a look at some of the last step-entrance buses that were working in London into the 21st century.

London Central's AV3 (M83MYM) an Alexander Royale bodied Volvo Olympian, approaches Canada Water in 2002. Not the most attractive bus, it was new to London in May 1995. Route 381 came into operation shortly before the turn of the century and is essentially a renumbered version of the P11.

Departing West Croydon in July 2001 is Arriva's C26CHM, a Leyland Olympian with Eastern Coach Works bodywork. Running between Brixton and Croydon, step entrance buses officially finished on route 109 in February 2001, but as this photo shows, they made the occasional trip well after that date.

London's Buses in the 21st Century

Cherished registration 166CLT, originally on RM1166, was carried by London General's Alexander Royale bodied Volvo Olympian when photographed approaching Putney Bridge Station in 2002. Later that year route 74 was withdrawn between Putney and Roehampton, that section being covered by new route 430. Both routes converted to low-floor buses at the same time.

At Kingston, working for London United (Westlink) in 2002 is AV27 (R927WOE), an Alexander bodied Volvo Olympian. After a spell with London & Country during the 1990s, route 57 has remained with London United. It converted fully to low-floor ALX400s in January 2003.

Metroline's superb Alexander bodied Scanias were initially in use on express route X43. At first the route was operated from Holloway garage, before being transferred to Potters Bar, where these Scanias joined others already in use from that garage on route 263. When this photo was taken in 2002 the X43 was history, and the Scanias could be found usually on commercial routes 84 and 242. Unusually, S13 (J813HMC) is working route 231 at Turnpike Lane, a route which would convert fully to low-floor Presidents in June 2003.

43

Alexander bodied Volvo Citybus F126PHM was new to the Cowie Group, for use by Grey-Green on its London routes. In 2002 it awaits departure from Leytonstone station. Cowie was renamed Arriva in 1997. After a short spell between 2003 and 2010 with Blue Triangle, route 66 returned to the Arriva fold on 4th September 2010, albeit operated by Arriva Southend from Grays garage.

The Leyland Titan was almost extinct in London in 2002. Here, London Central's B90WUV pulls away from Canada Water bus station working on route 381. London's last Titan was London Central's T1018 which carried on running until 19th June 2003.

London's Buses in the 21st Century

Lives of Leyland Nationals were extended by receiving new bodies by East Lancs. Known as 'Greenways' these hideous looking bodies were simply not pleasing on the eye, given how attractive the original Leyland National bodies were. London General's GUW479W shows it's rather bland body to good effect at Waterloo in 2001 on route 501. A former limited stop Red Arrow route, the 501 was withdrawn in 2002.

Northern Counties bodied Dennis Darts were less common on the streets of the capital than their Plaxton bodied cousins, but London Northern did acquire a batch in the summer of 1994. DNL115 (L115HHV) passes through Camden Town in 2002. In August 2003 this route received low-floor Darts.

45

Northern Counties bodied Volvo Olympian L213TWM was new to London Suburban Buses in 1994, before passing to London Northern when that company acquired LSB. In turn London Northern was to become part of Metroline. Route 4 converted to low-floor operation in April 2001. This shot was taken 10 months later, so obviously the odd step entrance bus was still making an appearance.

During 2002 Volvo Olympian P223MPU approaches Edmonton Green bus station. In 2005, First were to lose route W8 to Metroline. The W8 was originally part of the flat fare system of routes that led to the letter prefixes being used for the route. It was created in 1969 and was a direct replacement for the 128.

London's Buses in the 21st Century

I couldn't resist including a comparison section, a then and now feature. So via seven routes, here's what you could have seen, and what is operating now.

ROUTE MARCH

149

Route 149 was converted to Bendybus operation in 2004, and withdrawn at its northern end between Edmonton Green and Enfield garage at Ponders End. Arriva's MA12 (BX04MXK) arrives at Edmonton Green in July 2007. Initially the Bendybuses were garaged at Edmonton (EC) depot, but worked by crews from both EC and Stamford Hill (SF), however, early in 2005 the allocation was transferred to Lea Valley (LV).

In October 2010, on renewal of the contract, the Bendybuses were withdrawn and replaced with new Wrightbus Gemini 2 double-decker vehicles, and the allocation was moved to Tottenham (AR) garage.

DW315 (LJ10CVB) illustrates the type at Edmonton Green during November 2011.

31

Route 31 has seen a variety of different vehicle types over the past 25 years, ranging from Routemasters, through Mercedes-Benz minibuses to Dennis Darts and finally back to double-decker operation in 2004. On 22nd May 2001 First's Marshall bodied Dennis Dart DM291 (T291JLD) loads at Camden Town.

Running between Camden Town and Notting Hill Gate, the route was extended to Shepherds Bush in December 2006 and further extended two years later to the new White City bus station. At Swiss Cottage, in July 2007, is VNW32373 (LK04HZC) a Wright bodied Volvo B7TL, heading for Camden Town in one of First's more attractive liveries.

London's Buses in the 21st Century

148

The 148 is a relatively young route, being introduced in October 2002 using London United's (later Transdev) TA class of Tridents. Initially running between Shepherds Bush Green and Camberwell Green with a PVR of seventeen, the route was extended in 2008 to the new bus station at White City, and now has a PVR of twenty-five. In July 2007, TLA3 (SN53EUJ) picks up at the Elephant & Castle.

In October 2009 the contract was renewed and the route converted to 100% Scania OmniCity operation. These operate from Shepherd's Bush garage. SP12 (YN56FBV) heads along Park Lane towards Marble Arch in May 2009.

298

The 298 went through a multi coloured phase for eleven years between 1986 and 1997, being operated by London Country, Grey Green and then Capital Citybus, before settling down with Arriva. Wright bodied DAF, DWL53 (LF52UOE) has just arrived at Cockfosters on 8th May 2010.

Sullivan Buses took over operation of route 298 from 4th February 2012, under contract to TfL, and the route is being operated from their base at South Mimms. A batch of six Alexander Dennis Enviro200 buses was acquired for the service, to cope with a peak vehicle requirement of five. In Waterfall Road, nearing its Arnos Grove destination, is the last of the batch numerically, AE16 (SB61SUL), ten days after taking over the route.

London's Buses in the 21st Century

Arriva's ageing DLA class of ALX400s have been the mainstay of the 279 since 1999 when the route was converted from Metrobus to low-floor operation. In June 2009, DLA26 (S226JUA), an Alexander bodied DAF that was new in 1998 looks resplendent at Waltham Cross on a bright summers day in June 2009.

279

Arriva's T class of Enviro400s has been slow to take hold of the route since its introduction in February 2012. On 22nd February 2012 T228 (LJ61CFY) depicts the new order just outside Waltham Cross, heading south on Hertford Road at its junction with Bullsmoor Lane.

12

London Central's Routemaster RML2529 (JJD529D) heads through the Elephant & Castle on 24th March 2002 working on route 12 bound for Peckham. Two and a half years later the Routemasters were withdrawn and replaced by Bendybuses, and this brought about a decrease in the PVR from 38 to 29.

Seven years after the Bendybuses were introduced, they were withdrawn and the route returned to double-decker bus operation, seeing a PVR increase from 31 to 41. New Wright bodied Gemini 2s with a Volvo B5L chassis were purchased for the route, including some Hybrids. One of the green machines, WHV7 (LJ61GXE) approaches Oxford Circus on the first day of the new contract on 5th November 2011.

London's Buses in the 21st Century

25

In the days of conventional low-floor double-decker operation, route 25 had a PVR of 30. This was to increase to 37 when Bendybuses were introduced, subsequently increasing further to 43 in December 2007. In January 2002, before the Bendys' arrival, First's W939ULL, an ALX400 bodied Dennis Trident heads along Oxford Street.

First lost the contract for the 25 to Stagecoach East London when it was converted to Bendybus operation in 2004. 23075 makes the turn from Ave Maria Lane into St Pauls Churchyard whilst on diversion on 19th September 2010.

The 25 returned to First when the Bendybuses were withdrawn in the summer of 2011, and this saw a substantial PVR increase to 59. Brand new Gemini 2s based at Lea Interchange are now allocated to the route. VN36102 (BJ11DSZ) arrives at Oxford Circus on 5th November 2011.

53

SNOW

The capital did not experience much snow during the first decade of the 21st century, until we reached 2007. The white stuff opens up more opportunities for the photographer and here is a small selection.

In February 2002 route 263 returned to Potters Bar garage, after being lost to Leaside some six years earlier. Inevitably snow will cause disruption to bus services and on 6th January 2010 Metroline's TE944 (LK09EKU) is on the stand at East Finchley station on a short working of route 263.

With a PVR of ten, route 491 links Waltham Cross with the North Middlesex Hospital. Arriva's Enviro200, ENL14 (LJ58AVY) trundles through the snow at Enfield Island Village on 18th December 2010.

London's Buses in the 21st Century

The present-day 121 route is totally different from when it was first introduced in 1947 but the allocation has always been from either Enfield (E) garage, or Palmers Green (AD). Nowadays Enfield garage operates the entire route, using ALX400 DAF buses. Arriva's DLA128 (V628LGC), which was new in 1999, makes its way around Enfield Island Village on 18th December 2010, at the end of its journey.

With the snow continuing to fall, DMS1 (R701MEW) departs Chase Farm Hospital on 6th February 2007. With a PVR of 8, the W9 is usually in the hands of Metroline's DSD class of Dennis Dart Pointers, although the occasional Enviro200 does appear.

55

Taken shortly after the previous photo, President TP359 (LR52KWA) awaits departure time at Chase Farm hospital. The W8 has a PVR of fourteen and serves numerous schools throughout the length of the route. It is, therefore, best avoided at school opening and closing times.

Battling with both traffic and the elements at St Stephens Church, Enfield, is Arriva's DLA17 (S217JUA), nearing the end of its journey in February 2007. The latest contract for the 329 was awarded in January 2006, and the route is currently on a two year extension.

London's Buses in the 21st Century

TP407 (LK03CEX), approaches Enfield Town in February 2007. The W8 returned to Potters Bar in 2003 after a period with First, and the contract was renewed in 2010 following a two year extension in 2008.

The morning run-out from Potters Bar garage on 6th February 2007 and TP427 (LK03CGU) prepares to venture out into the cold, heading empty to Waltham Cross to start work on route 217. The garage at Potters Bar sits out on a limb, with no TfL routes operating to or from the garage in service. Instead these routes clock up a substantial amount of dead mileage running to and from their various starting/finishing points.

57

DARTING AROUND

The Dennis Dart, in its many guises, has been serving the capital for over 20 years. Here is a selection.

DDL15 (S315JUA) was delivered new to Arriva London South in 1998. Since then it has moved to Arriva the Shires and is now numbered 3218. This style of body, the Pointer built by Plaxton, is the most common used on the Dart chassis.

First's Marshall bodied Dart, DM41780 (X513HLR) built in 2001, collects passengers in Enfield Town in October. Showing a destination of Crews Hill Station, this route has now been cut back to Rosewood Drive, short of the station. Even more strange for a London bus route is that on weekdays there are only four return journeys, departing Enfield at hourly intervals from 1105 until 1405, although there are an extra three journeys on Saturdays.

London's Buses in the 21st Century

This 1996 built Dart Pointer P918PWW arrives at West Croydon in July 2001. The 450 was introduced in 1993, serving both north and south Croydon, although the present day route differs from the original by linking West Croydon with Sydenham through Crystal Palace. The Dart is now working for Arriva in North Wales.

Just a few minutes away from its terminus at Edmonton Green, Arriva's Dart Pointer PDL104 (LJ54BBO) heads along Victoria Road on 26th February 2011, the route having just changed hands from First to Arriva. This Dart was built in 2005.

The history of route 39 can be traced, in various forms, to 1950. Converted from double-decker operation to Mini buses in 1990, things had improved slightly by 2002 when this shot of London General's M207EGF crossing Putney Bridge was taken. Today the 39 has a PVR of 15. This Pointer was delivered in 1995.

Although it may seem strange to some of us today, some previously double-decker operated routes in the Enfield area lost their Metrobus allocation in favour of Dennis Darts in the late 90s. New in August 1996, Plaxton bodied Dennis Dart LDR24 (P824RWU) looks out of place on route 307 in Enfield in May 2000. Today the route is still in the hands of Arriva, with a PVR of 14, using President double-deckers once again, having converted in 2002.

London United (Transdev) operates route H22, using Dennis Dart SLFs, with a weekday PVR of 11 and 12 on Saturdays. At Hounslow bus station on 5th June 2010 is DPS672 (LG02FHB). This one has the Pointer 2 style body and is one of the buses built by Transbus, which had been created in 2001 by the merger of Dennis, Alexander and Plaxton.

London's Buses in the 21st Century

Caetano's Nimbus bodies were exclusively used on the Dart chassis and were built between 1999 & 2007. HV02OZU picks up at Loughton station in December 2001. The name Docklands Buses disappeared from the streets of London when the company was acquired by London General in 2006, although the history of the company can be traced back to Docklands Transit formed in 1993.

The Marshall Capital body was typically but not exclusively, placed on the Dart chassis. They were built between 1997 and 2003. Marshall closed in 2002 and the design for the body was bought by MCV but they only built five on the Dart chassis before Transbus stopped supplying them with the Dart Chassis. A 1998 built DML532 (R632VEG) passes through Enfield Town in 2003.

Alexander introduced the ALX200 body in 1996. It was built on the Volvo B6LE and the Dart chassis. With the creation of Transbus it was phased out in 2001. ADL5 (W605VGJ) collects passengers at Turnpike Lane in 2002. The ALX200 is rapidly disappearing from London.

61

A 1994 built Northern Counties Paladin bodied Dart L122YVK at the start of its journey on route 192 in May 2000. The body continued to be produced until 1998, 3 years after Plaxton had taken over the company. The 192 was introduced on 10th September 1994 linking the residential areas between Enfield and Edmonton with Angel Road Tesco. The route was extended in 2001 to Tottenham Hale.

Our final shot shows the rather worn driver's cab area inside Metroline's 1999 built Plaxton Pointer 2, DLD109 (T49KLD), taken in February 2011. More than 10,000 Darts, in their various forms, were built.

London's Buses in the 21st Century

A section showing the variety of Double-Deck buses that have worked the Capital's streets since 2000.

DOUBLE-DECKERS

One of the 2,786 Routemasters that were built, RML2591(JJD591D) travels north along Islington High Street in January 2005. The RMs were first introduced to London in 1956. Just over three months after this photo was taken route 19 lost its Routemasters in favour of Wrighbus Pulsar Geminis on DAF chassis. On 31st March 2012 London General took over operation of the 19, operating from Stockwell garage, using standard and hybrid Gemini 2s with a PVR of 26.

Along with the Leyland Titan, the MCW Metrobus, built from 1977 to 1989, was a common sight on London's streets throughout the 80s and 90s. The days of the type were numbered when B276WUL was photographed in Wood Green during 2002. This one was withdrawn in January 2004 and was scrapped later that year.

This Northern Counties Palatine bodied Leyland Olympian G546VBB was new to Kentish Bus in February 1990. The company was subsequently sold to British Bus and then Cowie/Arriva, By the time this photo was taken at Penge in February 2003 the bus was in Arriva livery. The Olympians came off this service in 2004.

Eastern Coach Works updated the Bristol VR body for use with the Leyland Olympian chassis. Two hundred and sixty three were ordered by London Buses. One of these, C58CHM, pulls away from West Croydon in 2001. Arriva operated the route from its Beddington Farm garage until its recent closure when it was transferred to the company's Croydon garage.

London's Buses in the 21st Century

This Alexander R type bodied, Volvo B10M, F136PHM was delivered new to the Cowie Group for Grey-Green's operations on the London Bus network in the 1990s. It was looking rather shabby in Pimlico in March 2002. Arriva lost this route in November 2002 with Metroline Presidents taking over.

S848DGX, an East Lancs bodied Volvo Olympian runs through East Croydon in July 2001. Metrobus continue to operate this service using Scania OmniCitys from its Croydon garage. This Olympian now runs as an open-topped sightseeing bus in Liverpool.

65

Stagecoach East London's R162VPU, an Alexander RL bodied Volvo Olympian, loads at Wood Green in 2002. These buses lasted on this route until 2006, when the route was won by First and Presidents took over, operated from Northumberland Park garage. First sold the garage and its routes to Go-Ahead in March 2012.

The Alexander bodied ALX400 was introduced in 1997 and production ceased in 2006. It has been fitted to a variety of types of chassis. TA246 (LG02FBO) is on a Dennis Trident chassis and awaits its departure time at Ealing in April 2009.

London's Buses in the 21st Century

A Plaxton President bodied Trident TNL33016 (LK51UYT) runs through Walthamstow. Like the ALX400, this was available on more than one type of chassis. This one, introduced in 2001, is on a Trident chassis. The President body was unveiled in 1997 and was in production from 1999 to 2005.

Hackney Community Transport, trading as CT Plus, runs route 388 between Hackney Wick and Embankment Station, on behalf of London Buses (TfL). HTL5 (LR52LWE) is a Trident with an East Lancs Myllennium Lolyne body and in June 2007 is on a short working to Liverpool Street Station.

Another of those rather cumbersome looking East Lancs bodies, the Myllennium Vyking, this time on a Volvo B7TL, working for London General at Kingston in 2002. EVL7 (PL51LGJ), along with the other EVLs within the fleet, have now all gone from London General.

SEL743 (LK07BAA) an East Lancs Olympus bodied N230UD Scania, passes Childs Hill in April 2010, Introduced in 2006, this body replaced the OmniDekka on the Scania chassis. The body has also replaced the Myllennium Vyking on the Volvo chassis and the Myllennium Lolyne on the Trident chassis.

London's Buses in the 21st Century

A Wrighbus Eclipse Gemini on a Volvo B7TL chassis, VLW176 (LJ03MPV) crosses Holloway Road bound for Euston on route 253 in May 2010. Although the vast majority have the Volvo chassis, a DAF/VDL version is also in operation and these are known as Pulsar Geminis.

The development of the Gemini is the Gemini 2. VW1043 (LK10BXM) was new in March 2010 and is captured from the top deck of another Gemini 2 in June 2010. The Gemini 2s can be purchased on the Volvo B9TL chassis or as an integral bus utilising VDL components.

69

The most common type of double-decked bus running in London in 2012 is the Alexander Dennis Enviro400 which utilises an updated Trident chassis. Over 1,000 have entered service since 1996. E95 (LX08ODS) passes the Hilton Hotel in Park Lane in June 2010.

The Scania OmniCity is built in Poland. Initially supplied on the N94UD chassis, it has since changed to the N230UD chassis. One of the latter versions, SP136 (YP59ODS) passes the BBC Television Centre in Wood Lane in June 2010.

London's Buses in the 21st Century

The move to reduce emissions has seen the development of hybrid technology. Wrightbus and Alexander Dennis have both had hybrid double-deckers in operation since 2008. WNH39005 (LK58ECZ), a Wright bodied Gemini 2 HEV arrives at Golders Green in April 2010.

Alexander Dennis has a hybrid version of the Enviro400 in operation - the 400H. TEH919 (LK58CPV) heads around Marble Arch towards Victoria in September 2011. The first batches of hybrids were finished in this leaf livery, but more recent arrivals are now all over red with the legend 'hybrid' subtly applied in green.

MARBLE ARCH

Come rain or shine Marble Arch is always a good place to photograph a variety of buses at work. Being basically a very large roundabout there are a number of vantage points to view the action.

Stagecoach East London's 17520 (LX51FNZ), an ALX400 bodied Dennis Trident that was delivered in 2001, heads along the northern side of Marble Arch past Edgware Road and is about to enter Oxford Street en route for Hackney Wick in 2009.

A pair of Routemasters RML2367 (JJD367D) on route 10 and RML2384 (JJD384D) on route 6, enter Oxford Street. RML2367 would have traversed three sides of Marble Arch having run up Park Lane from Hyde Park Corner, whereas RML 2384 has run down Edgware Road.

London's Buses in the 21st Century

A photo that depicts how busy Marble Arch is, seen from the eastern side looking towards Oxford Street. Scania OmniCity SP132 (YT59PCF) leads a Volvo ALX400, VLA154 (LJ55BRX) a Gemini 2, DW289 (LJ59LVU) and an unidentified Gemini.

No collection of photos of Marble Arch would be complete without a Bendybus. London Central's MAL38 (BD52LNP) skirts the south side on 20th February 2002. Route 436 was to lose its Bendybuses in November 2011 in favour of Enviro400s.

73

The original route 23 was incorporated into route 15 in May 1985, leaving London without a route 23 until the present route was introduced in July 1992. Currently operated from Westbourne Park with a PVR of 30, First's Trident ALX400 TNA33359 (LK53EXX) heads down the east side in September 2010.

In November 2009 route 113 was altered at Selfridges to terminate at Marble Arch rather than its existing termination point of Oxford Circus. With its destination blind already set for its return journey, TE840 (LK57AXV), is seen in September 2010.

London's Buses in the 21st Century

A Dart Pointer, KU52YKZ was new to Thorpes in 2002 as DLF104. Seen here working on route 705, the route linked Paddington to London Liverpool Street, taking in other mainline stations at Victoria, Waterloo, London Bridge and Fenchurch Street.

Dart Pointer 2, DLD698 (LK55KLO) heads from Marble Arch into Oxford Street in 2009. The new edict from TfL that buses must be painted all-over red, means that this distinctive livery is now being phased out.

75

Not surprisingly the London sightseeing buses feature Marble Arch on their tours of the capital. One of The Big Bus Company's Alexander bodied tri-axle Leyland Olympian MBO354 (E354NUV) stands out of service on the east side as an Eclipse Gemini WVL199 (LX05EZR) slips past into Park Lane.

Arriva's The Original Tour's tri-axle, dual door MCW Metrobus EMB765 (E965JAR) heads for Park Lane. This bus was built in 1988 for use by China Motor Bus in Hong Kong. The bus was sold to Arriva and brought back to Britain in 2000.

London's Buses in the 21st Century

Trident President TPL253 (LN51KYJ) heads to North Finchley. Metroline started a new five year contract on this route in March 2012 and it is planned that the Presidents will be replaced by new buses on this route by early 2013.

Routemaster buses did not last long on route 390. The 390 was the last route to be provided with Routemasters, but these only lasted until 3rd September 2004, when the route was converted to OPO. RML2413 (JJD413D) waits at the stand in Tyburn Way in the centre of the Marble Arch roundabout in February 2002.

77

GOLDEN JUBILEE

In 2012 Her Majesty Queen Elizabeth II celebrated her Diamond Jubilee. Ten years earlier, fifty buses across London received this gold livery for her Golden Jubilee.

Fifteen Routemasters received the gold treatment. First's RM1650 (650DYE) heads along Oxford Street in August 2002. Just over a year later Route 23 lost its Routemaster Buses in favour of low-floor OPO double-deckers.

London United's ALX400 Trident TA225 (SN51SZU) waits on the stand at Kingston, in between journeys in April 2002. There were five sponsors of the fifty buses, each with ten buses. Whilst the front and sides of these buses were gold, they featured adverts on the back.

London's Buses in the 21st Century

TfL was one of the sponsors and one of its ten was Metroline's Volvo B7TL President VPL163 (Y163NLK) seen leaving Hampstead Road on a short working of route 134 to Warren Street in August 2002. In 1948 the 134 ran between Potters Bar and Pimlico. Now its southern end terminates at Tottenham Court Road Station whilst to the north it has moved off course slightly to finish at North Finchley. The 134 provides a 24 hour service, with a mix of low-floor double-decker types, and is operated from Holloway (HT) garage with a PVR of 32.

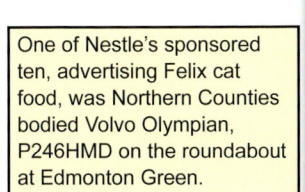

One of Nestle's sponsored ten, advertising Felix cat food, was Northern Counties bodied Volvo Olympian, P246HMD on the roundabout at Edmonton Green.

79

I like this photo of Arriva's Volvo Olympian H157XYU, working Arriva's Volvo Olympian H157XYU. Sponsored by Unilever and advertising Surf washing powder, it picks up in New Oxford Street on 14th April 2002. The official launch of the gold buses did not take place until 2nd May 2002 with one bus from each sponsor being posed for photos in Trafalgar Square.

Displaying 'Congratulations on your wedding day', rather odd for the Queen's Golden Jubilee, is London Central's RML2283 (CUV283C) heading through Waterloo on 2nd August 2002. This one was sponsored by Mars and was advertising Celebrations sweets.

London's Buses in the 21st Century

Over a month before the official launch Stagecoach's RML2450 (JJD450D) was already finished in gold without any advertising. A few of the RMs ran without adverts for a short while after the official launch.

First Centrewest's Trident President T832LLC was one of the ten sponsored by Marks & Spencer and is seen here in Marylebone Road on 2nd August 2002. Route 18 succumbed to the Bendybus craze in 2003 but normality resumed seven years later when, in 2010, low-floor double-deckers returned.

81

SINGLE-DECKERS

A section showing the variety of single-deck buses that have worked the capital's streets since 2000.

DML528 (R638VEG), a Marshall bodied Dennis Dart during the Spring of 2000. The bus station at Waltham Cross was being redesigned at this time and buses were departing from these temporary stops on the opposite side of the main shopping area.

The driver of this Dennis Dart East Lancs Spryte DE415 (V337MBV) looks for a parking space at Brent Cross in November 2006. This Spryte was new to Wings Buses in 1999, Wings was subsequently taken over by Telling Golden Miller which was, in turn, taken over by Travel London which was then taken over by Abellio. The route remains with Abellio today.

London's Buses in the 21st Century

London United's Plaxton Pointer bodied Dennis Dart DPS557 (Y557XAG) arrives at Kingston at the end of its journey in 2002.

HDC11 (X595ORV) a Caetano Nimbus bodied Dennis Dart runs along Holloway Road in February 2009. This is one of eleven operated by CT Plus since 2001.

Alexander ALX200 bodied Dennis Dart, SLD304 (LX51FGF) runs through Brixton in 2002. This route is still operated by Stagecoach from Catford garage with a PVR of 10.

Caetano Nimbus bodied Dennis Dart 8490 (KX03HZS) at Ealing Common. Note the air conditioning unit on the roof. This bus was delivered new to Ealing Community Transport in 2003 but when it stopped trading as a bus operator in 2009 Abellio acquired this bus.

East Lancs Myllennium bodied Scania, ELS10 (YR52VFH) heads onto Tower Bridge in December 2010. This bus had been bought for use on the government (TfL) East Thames Buses services in 2002 and worked for them until the company was sold to Go-Ahead in 2009.

London's Buses in the 21st Century

MCV Evolution bodied Dart, ED10 (AE56OUJ) at Loughton in Docklands Buses livery although the company had been sold to Go-Ahead just before this bus was delivered. Go-Ahead still operate this route but it is through the Blue Triangle subsiduary and not Docklands.

While we are looking at single-deck buses, let us not forget a route to the very north of London that, although not a full London bus route, did accept London tickets over the section between Enfield and Waltham Cross. Linking Hertford with North London were Arriva's routes 310 & 311. 3418 (P418HVX), a Wright bodied Dennis Dart that was new to County Bus & Coach, is seen in the small bus station in Enfield Town in 2002. Today the route no longer reaches Enfield, terminating at the TfL boundary at Waltham Cross.

85

Route 268 is operated by Arriva the Shires from its premises in Watford which explains the four digit fleet number, as opposed to the more traditional numbering used by Arriva in London. 3716 (YE06HRJ) is seen at Golders Green in December 2010.

Passing through Cricklewood in September 2011 is MM810 (LK57AYD) an MCV Evolution bodied MAN 12.240. Introduced in 2007, Metroline is the only operator with this type of bus, running thirty-eight of them.

London's Buses in the 21st Century

The Enviro200 is rapidly becoming the single-decker of choice for London operators. One of the more recent arrivals is ENX3 (LJ61CKK) pictured heading out of Potters Bar on 19th November 2011. The Enviros have replaced DAF Wrightbus Cadets on route 313.

Devoid of operator names, this photo was taken on 5th June 2010, in Wood Lane. It features Enviro200, ADL31 (SK07DYU) which had been delivered new to NCP Challenger (later known as NSL Buses) in 2007. NSL was sold to Transdev in 2009.

87

Optare Versa 25314 (LX09AAN) passes through Gants Hill in March 2012. This is one of fourteen Versas operated by Stagecoach, five of which are based at Barking for working route 396 alongside Enviro200s. The other nine are at Plumstead for route 469.

Bringing the story right up to date is the Wrightbus Streetlite. WS2 (LJ12CGG) passes Gants Hill underground station on 24th March 2012. Operated by Go-Ahead Blue Triangle the Streetlifes have replaced Arriva Darts on route 462.

London's Buses in the 21st Century

As well as hybrid double-deckers, hybrid single-deckers run in London. This is Optare Tempo OTH974 (LK09EKG) on the Uxbridge road in December 2011. This is one of five Hybrid Tempos operated by Metroline.

First's WSH62993 (LK60HPJ) heads across Waterloo Bridge in April 2011. This is one of the Wrightbus hydrogen fuel cell buses that emit zero emissions. Five are based at Lea Interchange for use on RV1. Introduction to service started in early 2011 and some teething problems have been experienced, sometimes resulting in none being available for service.

LONDON'S OLYMPIANS

In 1984, London Buses set up an evaluation trial to test different types of vehicle with a view to their next purchase of double-deck buses. Involving three Volvo Ailsas, three Dennis Dominators, two Mark II Metrobuses and three Leyland Olympians, it was the Olympian that was chosen, and delivery commenced in the early part of 1986. Bodied initially by Eastern Coach Works (ECW) at Lowestoft, other bodies later became available. The following photos offer a selection of views of the Olympian at work on London's streets during the first three years of the 21st century.

Differing body styles can be seen here at Euston in 2003. To the left is L243 (D243FYM) carrying the familiar ECW bodywork, whilst about to depart for Hackney on route 253 is L317 (J317BSH) an Alexander bodied example that was new in April 1992.

L247 (D247FYM) at Penge in February 2003. New in January 1987, it is working route 312 which had allegedly converted to low-floor operation two years earlier.

London's Buses in the 21st Century

London Central's NV86 (R286LGH) was new in February 1998 and had Northern Counties Palantine bodywork. It was only two years old when seen passing under the rail bridge at Waterloo. Today it can be found painted yellow working in the North East.

First's Volvo Olympian S219LLO had a Northern Counties Palatine body and was new to Capital Citybus in October 1998. It is seen here passing through Euston bus station in 2002. Later that year this route was converted to low-floor Presidents and this bus is now working in Sheffield for First.

Armchair's R419SOY arrives at Kingston in 2002. This bus carries the more unusual style of Northern Counties Palatine 2 bodywork. Shortly after this photo was taken the bus moved to the North West of England.

One of the earlier examples delivered in April 1986 was L66 (C66CHM). Here it passes through Brixton in 2002.

After Leyland closed the ECW factory in Lowestoft in 1987, production moved to Leyland's plant at Workington. Bodies were produced in a style similar to those provided by ECW, but the Olympians were now 'all Leyland' so to speak. L303 (G303UYK) was part of a batch acquired by London Buses for route 237 (Sunbury Village to Shepherds Bush Green) and carried Riverbus fleetnames. Late in 2002, L303, along with sister L308, moved to Edgware as spares for the BTS routes, which included route 13. Carrying Sovereign as its fleetname, later known as 'London Sovereign', L303 is about to enter Oxford Street at Oxford Circus in 2003.

London's Buses in the 21st Century

London United's Alexander bodied Volvo Olympian VA7 (N137YRW) loads at Kingston bound for Epson on route 406 in 2002. Surprisingly this and four other VAs are still based at London United's Fulwell garage and are available for hire through their commercial department.

Alexander Royal bodywork is fitted on this Volvo Olympian, N130YRW, which heads along Marylebone Road on Airbus route A2 in 2002. Popularity of the Airbus routes fell at the turn of the century, following the introduction of the Heathrow Express rail service and the various Airbus services were either withdrawn or sold over the following years. The bus moved to the south west, working in Devon & Cornwall for First.

93

New in October 1993 to London Suburban, L210SKD ended its London days working for Metroline. In 2002 it aproaches Waterloo on route 4. After leaving Metroline the bus was moved north and is now operated by Geldards in Leeds.

L38 (C38CHM) is given a second life with Arriva outside of London. Taken at Enfield Town in 2002, this ECW bodied Leyland Olympian was new in March 1986 and was transferred from Arriva London South to Arriva East Herts & Essex in 2002. Today it is named Beryl and has been converted to a luxury camper by the Bespoke Bus Company.

London's Buses in the 21st Century

In the first twelve years of the 21st Century the 38 has gone from Routemaster, through OPO double-deckers on Sundays, Bendybuses, to OPO double-deckers full time and now almost back to Routemasters with the crew operated New Bus for London. These photos depict the changes.

'38' CHANGES

By 2000 the route was running from Victoria to Clapton Pond. RM2185 (CUV185C) stands in Victoria bus station in 2000. Routemasters had been plying their trade on the 38 since their introduction to the route in 1971 and survived for thirty-four years.

In line with all London's crew-operated routes, to save costs Sunday services were converted to OPO operation during 1987, initially using Titans from Leyton (T) garage. In 2002 Alexander bodied Olympian J352BSH makes a stop in Islington High Street.

95

Mercedes-Benz Citaro articulated buses came to the 38 in October 2005, replacing the Routemasters and lasting just four years until November 2009. MA81 (BU05VFE) crosses the traffic lights at the end of Islington High Street on 28th July 2007. These buses were garaged at Ash Grove but the route was still administered from Clapton (CT).

Double-deck OPO buses returned to the 38 on 14th November 2009, bringing about a huge jump in the PVR from 42 to 70. At Victoria bus station on the first day of the new operation is Gemini 2, DW241 (LJ59AEN).

London's Buses in the 21st Century

Mixed operations sees Enviro400s sometimes working alongside the DW's. Arriva's T70 (LJ59ADX) departs Victoria bus station for Hackney Central.

The first of the 'New Bus for London' buses are to enter service on the route and are capable of being either crew or OPO operated. Not yet given an official name they are generally known, by enthusiasts at least, as the 'Borismaster'. LT1 (LT61AHT) was shown to the public prior to the type entering service, and is seen at Golders Green on 6th January 2012, although LT2 was actually the first one to enter service on 27th February 2012. Whether they will become the new face of London buses pretty much depends on politics.

97

TRAINING

Driver training buses are usually buses that have previously been used in service and adapted for their new role. They tend to be older types thus adding more variety to the London scene.

Metrobus M1405 (C405BUV) is in Arriva's all white training livery at Edmonton Green on 6th May 2008. Having been delivered in 1985 it ran in service until June 2004, when it was designated a trainer. Days after this photo was taken it was sold for scrap.

Slightly more modern is LF02PNY, a Wright bodied DAF seen on training duties in Enfield in April 2011.

London's Buses in the 21st Century

A little out of its usual operating area, London United's MAN 11.190 Optare Vecta, MV6 (N286DWY) pauses on Enfield Highway on 9th February 2011. This was built in 1985 and transferred from the Midlands to London United at the end of the last century.

Metroline does not have a dedicated livery for its training vehicles. DLD202 (LN51KXH) a 2002 Transbus built Dart Pointer passes under the bridge at Brondesbury station in December 2010.

Departing from Arriva's Tottenham garage is M787 (KYV787X), wearing a rather striking livery against crime for the Metropolitan Police, in May 2002. It was converted to training use in 2001 after 19 years in service. It was sold for scrap a year after this photo was taken.

Not all training vehicles are driver trainers. Metroline's 'Learning on the Move' bus was linked to the learning centres based in some garages enabling staff to further their education on matters not related to bus driving. At Potters Bar garage on 11th March 2008 is M151 (33 LUG), previously registered as BYX151V when delivered new to London Transport in 1979.

London's Buses in the 21st Century

First's Metrobus M1328 (C328BUV) looks resplendent in this view at Wembley Park on 6th January 2007. After a period of two and a half years in store it became a trainer in June 2000, a role it performed until September 2007.

Metroline's KU52YKZ is a Dart Pointer 2 that was delivered new to Thorpes of Wembley in 2002. It received this pink livery for awareness of Breast Cancer, and was photographed at Potters Bar on 11th March 2008. Metroline purchased Thorpes of Wembley in 2005.

SIGHTSEEING

The sightseeing circuit has added plenty of variety to the bus scene in London.

Offering 'luxury sightseeing' according to the wording on the front, is Arriva's M633 (KYV633X) a Metrobus that was new to London Transport in 1981. In 2000 it had part of the roof removed and entered service with The Original London Sightseeing Tour (TOLST). In this photo, taken in 2002, it awaits customers at Victoria. Today it is owned by Ensignbus and was used at Showbus 2011 as the show control vehicle.

Leyland Titans were also common on sightseeing work in London during the nineties and into the 'noughties'. T384 (KYV384X) was delivered to London Transport in 1981. It was bought by The Big Bus Company in 1999 and had its roof removed. Here it passes Tower Hill Station in 2002.

London's Buses in the 21st Century

Arriva's M509 (GYE509W) is seen here working through Victoria in 2002 for their City Sightseeing London operation. It was converted to open-top in July 1998 and remained on sightseeing trips until 2005.

TOLST's MXT179 is a tri-axle 12 metre MCW Metrobus that was built in the UK for export to Hong Kong for China Motor Bus. After also working in Australia it returned to the UK in 2006 and is seen here earning its keep for Arriva on 19th September 2010.

ML12 (A112KFX) is a MCW Metroliner that was new to Shamrock and Rambler in 1984. It looks slightly out of place as it passes through Victoria in 2002. The yellow triangle in the front screen was used to denote which service it was working.

HELP!

Despite the best efforts of the engineering departments, buses do breakdown. If the operator's mechanics are not on hand, there is always Sovereign Recovery, who can if required tow the errant bus back to base.

The big red London Buses recovery truck lurks in central London and is used to attend any breakdowns speedily to help keep the streets free from obstruction. Belonging to Sovereign, GM03TOW is seen at its usual haunt just off Park Lane on 2nd June 2010.

Waterloo is the location for this view of Arriva's DLA299 (Y499UGC) receiving assistance having failed on route 243, despite what the rear blind states!

London's Buses in the 21st Century

An unidentified Dennis Dart belonging to First was photographed in Regents Park Road being towed on 25th August 2008. It takes around ten minutes for the tow truck driver to hitch his rig to a failed bus.

Before the recovery truck is called, fitters will try to remedy the problem. One of Potters Bar's finest engineers attends TP439 (LK03GGV) at Chase Farm Hospital on 5th June 2011.

Metroline's DMS25 (S525KFL) failed on Wades Hill whilst working route W9 on 7th December 2007. Once again Sovereign attend and the vehicle was later towed back to Potters Bar

105

METROBUSES

The Metrobus was a fine workhorse, serving the travelling public across London for twenty-six years. The first examples entered service in November 1978, and the type continued to ply the streets of the capital reliably until 2004, when the last Metrobuses were withdrawn.

Waterloo is the setting for this view of M1153 (B153WUL) at work on route 4 in 2001. Devoid of an operator name, it was in fact working for Metroline, although still in the all-over red livery of MTL London Northern which Metroline had taken over 3 years earlier.

A pair of Arriva Metrobuses play 'follow the leader' at Camden Town in May 2000 whilst working on route 29. At the front is M1278 (B278WUL) heading for Trafalgar Square, whilst the unidentified bus in the distance will be turned short at Tottenham Court Road. Metrobuses worked the route between 1992 and 2002 before their replacement by Tridents.

London's Buses in the 21st Century

M1031 (A731THV) was new in May 1984. Photographed at Victoria in 2001, it was a long way from its home garage of Potters Bar whilst working route 82. Metrobuses operated this route from December 1993 until September 2001, when Presidents took over.

London United's M1343 (C343BUV) heads through Kingston, bound for Chessington World of Adventures, on route 71 in the summer of 2002 just days before the Metrobuses were replaced by ALX400s. Metrobuses started on this route in August 1985 replacing Routemasters.

In 2000 route 149 was a lengthy route, running all the way from Enfield Garage to London Bridge, before being shortened when Bendybuses were introduced in 2004. Crossing London Bridge at the end of its journey is Arriva's M675 (KYV675X).

On a wet day in Muswell Hill in 2000, Arriva's M776 (KYV776X) works route 102. This route changed from Routemasters to Metrobuses in September 1982 and the type survived on it for twenty years before being replaced by Wrightbus Geminis.

London's Buses in the 21st Century

Climbing Muswell Hill at the end of its journey in 2000 is Metroline's M1058 (B58WUL) on route W7. A total of one thousand four hundred and forty Metrobuses were ordered for London between 1978 & 1985. An additional two prototypes of a mark 2 design were delivered in 1984, but no further orders were placed.

In the days before the Disability Discrimination Act, buses had neat and tidy lower saloons, with ample, 'comfortable' seats, unlike today's bucket-like seats with thin padding which are uncomfortable within twenty minutes of use. The lovely interior of a London Metrobus, with its brightly coloured seats, is shown to good effect in this view of M2.

109

In their declining years the Metrobuses in London were starting to look tired and worn. Metroline's M1339 (C339BUV) was not looking its best when captured by the camera at Golders Green in 2002 working route 240. It was however, in its seventeenth year of service! Presidents took over the following year.

Arriving at Enfield Town on route 329 in 2000 is Arriva's M692 (KYV692X). It entered service in January 1982 and lasted until May 2001 when it was sold for scrap.

M1231 (B231WUL) loads at Edmonton Green on route 149 in 2000. Following its withdrawal this bus became a training vehicle, it was eventually sold off to Ensignbus in July 2008, who sent it for scrap.

London's Buses in the 21st Century

A trio of Metroline Metrobuses stand in the rain back in May 2000 on the bus stand at Muswell Hill Broadway, awaiting their next journeys on route W7. The leading bus M1058 (B58WUL) survives today. It has had its roof removed and is operated by SS Suncruisers in sunny Scarborough.

In 2000 not all bus routes served the small bus station at Waltham Cross. Country routes used the paved area through the shopping area, as seen in this view of Metroline's M1151 (B151WUL) collecting passengers on route 310A.

111

HILL CLIMBING

Central London is not much higher than sea level, but the highest point to the south is Westerham Heights at an elevation of 245 metres. To the north Bushey Heath stands at 153 metres. There are, therefore, some interesting hills for London's buses to negotiate.

Making the climb up Osidge Lane in Southgate on 29th July 2009 is Arriva's Edmonton based PDL89 (LF52USJ), working on route 382. Dart Pointers have been used on the route since its inception in July 2003. In February 2012 the Darts were reallocated to Wood Green.

Muswell Hill stands at an elevation of 105 metres. Enviro400, T6 (LJ08CVX), climbs Alexandra Park Road into Muswell Hill on 6th May 2008. This is a Palmers Green based bus.

London's Buses in the 21st Century

PDL78 (LF52UOO) climbs Kings Head Hill into Chingford on route 379 on 21st September 2010. The 379 must be one of the shortest routes in London, its daytime running time being just twelve minutes. While this must be incredibly monotonous for the drivers, the route does provide an important link from the north west area of Chingford, into the centre.

With stunning views across London, albeit slightly hazy on this occasion, Metroline's VPL136 (X636LLX), a Plaxton bodied Volvo B7TL, completes its lengthy climb up the steep Muswell Hill at the end of its route W8 journey from Finsbury Park on 14th April 2011.

113

THE IRISH CONNECTION

Wrightbus, based in Ballymena Northern Ireland, first supplied buses to London in 1990 with the Dennis Dart chassied single-deck Handybus. They then pioneered the first low-floor bus, the Pathfinder in 1993 built on either Dennis Lance or Scania N113 chassis. However, it wasn't until 2001, when the Volvo B7TL chassied Eclipse Gemini was launched, that Wrightbus gained big orders for London. And of course today they are building the New Bus for London.

A bright summer's day on 2nd June 2010 as London General's WVL144 (LX53AYU) takes on board a large number of passengers on route 11 at Victoria. This Stockwell based bus was allocated to this route when the Routemasters were replaced in October 2003 and still works it today.

First's VNW32392 (LK04HXA) passes through Camden Town on 8th July 2007, working route 31 to Shepherds Bush. This bus was delivered new to the route in April 2004 and was part of the conversion from Marshall bodied Dennis Dart single-deckers to double-deckers.

London's Buses in the 21st Century

Stamford Hill based Eclipse Geminis work alongside Trident ALX400s on the 253. VLW195 (LJ53BEU) passes through Finsbury Park working the route on 12th November 2011. Seven hundred and thirteen of these Volvo powered buses were built for London, with another one hundred and thirty five with DAF chassis called Pulsar Geminis.

Route 343 started in February 2001 and was run by Go-Ahead with Volvo B7TL Presidents. Travel London, a National Express company, took over the route from February 2006 and used Geminis on the service, operating out of Walworth garage. 9029 (BX55XMP), heads for New Cross Gate on 19th July 2007 at the Elephant and Castle.

115

Our final look at an original Gemini is of Go-Ahead London's WVL148 (LX53AYZ) at Charing Cross, on 26th June 2004. Using London buses as moving billboards has been going on for years and with advancements in vinyl production it has become very easy to cover a whole bus. There is always a handful running round promoting something or other, even with the latest edict from London Buses that buses should be completely red. This is one such example, advertising 'The Lion King'.

In 2009 an updated version of the Gemini started to appear in London - the Gemini 2. It is supplied with a VDL DB300 chassis, known as an integral or with a Volvo B9TL chassis. This is one of the Volvos, VW1205 (LK61BMU) running on its first day of service on 26th November 2011 at Queensbury Station. On this day Metroline took over operation of route 79 from First which had used the mark one version of the Gemini on the service.

London's Buses in the 21st Century

Arriva's DW470 (LJ61CDF), an Integral Gemini 2, was one of the buses scheduled for use on route 29 when that route lost its Bendybuses at the end of November 2011. Shortly before that event, on 12th November 2011, it was used on route 141 and is seen pulling out of Wood Green garage. This newest batch of Gemini 2s have been built to comply with a new European design directive - European Community Whole Vehicle Type Approval (ECWVTA).

The 43 is a route close to my heart, being the first bus route I was to drive in London as a newly qualified bus driver back in 1986. Today the route operates around the clock, providing a 24 hour service from Metroline's Holloway (HT) garage with a PVR of 35. Having gained a two year extension in 2010, the 43 has just commenced a new five year contract and new Wright Gemini 2 Volvo B9TLs have started to be introduced, alongside existing Enviro400s and Tridents. On 7th April 2012 VW1243 (LK12AAF) departs the bus stand at its northern terminus in Friern Barnet bound for London Bridge.

On the single-decker front, the overwhelming choice for London from the mid-90s was the Dennis Dart chassied buses. However, Wrightbus did get some of the action. The Cadet utilised a DAF SB120 chassis and Arriva was the major customer for this type, the first arriving in 2001. DWL27 (LF02PMO) is about to enter the one-way system in Enfield Town on route 313 back in 2003. The Cadets worked this route from April 2002 to November 2011 when they were replaced by Enviro200s.

Although not officially allocated to this route at the time, DWL38 (LF02PNU) is seen at Potters Bar station in 2003, heading for the Cranborne Road industrial estate. However, in February 2007, they were allocated to the route and lasted until Enviro200s ousted them in February 2012. Wrightbus is making another effort to break the Enviro200s' growing dominance in the capital with their new Streetlite bus (see page 88) which is currently being trialed on London's streets.

London's Buses in the 21st Century